T0114946

BRIGITTA,
LITTLE GIRL OF THE ALLEGHENY MOUNTAINS

BOOK TWO

JUNIOR HIGH SCHOOL AND ONWARD

INGE LOGENBURG KYLER

authorHOUSE®

AuthorHouse™
1663 Liberty Drive
Bloomington, IN 47403
www.authorhouse.com
Phone: 833-262-8899

Published by AuthorHouse 06/02/2023

ISBN: 979-8-8230-0788-7 (sc)
ISBN: 979-8-8230-0791-7 (e)

Library of Congress Control Number: 2023908710

Print information available on the last page.

*Any people depicted in stock imagery provided by Getty Images are models,
and such images are being used for illustrative purposes only.
Certain stock imagery © Getty Images.*

This book is printed on acid-free paper.

This book is dedicated to my loving husband, Arthur J. Kyler, who was my junior high school sweetheart, and who has been supportive in all my endeavors throughout our life together.

Illustrations by Inge

Contents

Forward

Brigitta Grows Up follows follows Brigitta, Little Girl of the Allegheny Mountains.

As some people have guessed, the Brigitta stories are true accounts of Inge(Brigitta) and Betty (Mary) Logenburg, daughters of William and Marie, who were both born in Germany. Marie came to the U.S. with her mother and her sister Martha, and brothers Paul and Alfred. They boarded a steamship and crossed the Atlantic two weeks after the Titanic disaster. Originally, they had tried to book the Titanic but it was full, Marie's father Johann had already settled in Pennsylvania. William (or Bill) was sponsored by his Aunt Krause who lived in Munson, Pennsylvania. He was either 19 or 20 when he disembarked from a train in front of the St. Paul Lutheran German Church in Winburne, PA. Marie just happened to be in church that day. Her mother invited William to dinner, and that was that.

The Logenburg family lived in Wolf Run, near Clearfield, Pennsylvania until 1953 when they moved to Lansing, Michigan. Both Inge and Betty have fond memories of the beautiful mountains and farmlands of Pennsylvania. When Inge's family was grown, Inge and her husband spent many delightful summer vacations in Cabin No. 1 in Black Moshannon State Park.

The name Brigitta seemed easier to pronounce than Inge as all through her life, no one seemed able to pronounce it. Inge wants readers to know that she had wonderful loving parents who indulged her passion to study dance even though money was still tight from the Great Depression.

Note: Names of many of the people mentioned in the following story have been changed, but Clearfield is a real town in central Pennsylvania. Brigitta's home became abandoned through the years and only pieces of it might still remain, buried forever behind motels, hotels, gas stations and other buildings constructed in a world that forever changes.

Chapter 1

A New Adventure

Junior High! What a scary place that seemed to be! Now it was time to say goodbye to grammar school friends and move on into a bigger world of unfamiliar faces.

The best part of going onward meant that Brigitta no longer had to walk a mile or so to catch the school bus to grammar school. Now she could wait for the bus at the mail box at the end of the long driveway from their little house down in the valley. The bus schedule was erratic, to say the least, and Brigitta knew she had to be there early or she might miss it.

On rainy days she pulled rubber galoshes over her shoes to protect them before she could walk down the long and sometimes muddy driveway. None of her classmates liked to wear boots to school. Once Brigitta reached the mailbox, she pulled off the boots and stuffed them in, hoping the mailman would be understanding. Fortunately for her, he never complained. Also, it was a good thing that the mailbox was large enough to hold a pair of boots.

The junior high school building was a three-story wooden structure in downtown Clearfield around the corner from the Ritz Theatre and the main shopping center. Students were not allowed to venture downtown during their lunch hour, however. They had to remain on campus.

It was such an old building that there were a lot of fire drills, which meant rushing down the stairs and onto the sidewalk and street.

There was no air conditioning either, but windows were allowed to be opened on stuffy days.

Students were assigned homerooms where they would go first thing in the morning and last thing in the afternoon. Brigitta didn't know any of the other students in her homeroom and for a number of days she felt quite lost. Being a consolidated school meant students came from all over the county. She had no idea what happened to some of her grammar school friends. However, she had heard that a couple of the bigger boys from Plymptonville Elementary School had talked about quitting school as soon as they could and, maybe they had, as she didn't see any of them in the crowded junior high school building.

The school had a dress code. Girls had to wear dresses or skirts and blouses. Many students wore black and white saddle shoes. Brigitta didn't care for them. She much preferred the daintier black shoes that looked like ballerina slippers, befitting a prospective ballerina, which she aspired to be. Boys were told they had to dress neatly.

Rather than staying in one room all day like they did in grammar school, students moved from room to room for different classes. When the bell rang, it was time to change classes, and students filed into the busy hallways. It was easy to feel intimidated by the big eighth graders. Brigitta felt like she was on a brand new adventure, and, in a sense, she was.

Chapter 2

Changes, Changes, Changes

Brigitta's Grandmother Lipka on her mother's side died in the middle of summer. She had been living in Michigan but when she became sick, she wanted to be with Brigitta's mother in Pennsylvania. She was very ill when she arrived by bus. The doctor said she did not have long to live. She slept in Brigitta's parents' bedroom where she moaned in pain most of every night. It was very distressing for everyone.

One day that June, Brigitta was sent to spend the day with her girlfriend Ellen in Plymptonville. While she was there, another friend stopped by and said she had just seen the funeral hearse at Brigitta's house, so Brigitta knew her grandmother had died. She felt sad and yet knew that now her grandmother no longer had to suffer in pain.

Aunts and uncles came from out of town to stay with Brigitta's family for the funeral. Since all the beds and couches were taken, Brigitta ended up putting blankets in the bathroom bathtub so she would have a place to sleep.

Grandmother was buried in an old German cemetery on top of a steep hill in Winburne behind the vacant St. Paul Lutheran Church on Sawmill Road. Grandmother, many years ago, had been a Sunday School teacher at the church while Grandfather was the choir master. But over the years the congregation moved away or died and the church was closed and boarded up.

The evening following the funeral Brigitta had to go to the junior high school to be on the radio with her 4-H group. The group was scheduled to do a special program. It was very late when she finally got home. The next day, all of the relatives left for their homes. Later in the week Brigitta and her mother went to the movies to see "To The Ends of The Earth." It felt good to be doing something happy.

The rest of that summer was very hot. On the hill the water reservoir that was their source of running water for the house went dry. This was the first time this had ever happened. The reservoir was a deep hole that her father had dug soon after he built the house. He had laid pipes from the reservoir down the hill to the house. Now that it had dried up, they had to scoop water out of the creek in the woods until rains finally came and filled up the reservoir again.

It was during this time that Brigitta's sister, Mary, went to York in eastern Pennsylvania to attend business school to be a legal secretary. She would stay with a family to help with chores and babysitting in exchange for room and board while attending college.

Suddenly the little bedroom that Brigitta shared with her sister seemed quiet and empty. They had both shared the same bed and now it seemed cold and lonely. Brigitta started having nightmares from being in that little room all by herself. She pulled the covers over her face and tried to sleep.

This was not an easy adjustment as Brigitta missed her sister and missed how, when they washed the dishes in the kitchen, they used to pretend to be Mrs. Brown and Mrs. Twiddle. Now she would have to do dishes all by herself. It didn't seem much fun being Mrs. Twiddle without her sister around to be Mrs. Brown.

She also missed no longer seeing her sister's boyfriends who used to drive down the long driveway to visit. Her dad, however, probably did not miss having to get out of bed during the night to help get cars unstuck in the snow in the winter. When that happened, he had to get a bucket of ashes from the coal furnace and scatter it on the road and under the car wheels to give the wheels traction. Then the boyfriend would be able to back out of the ruts in the snowy roads.

Brigitta's sister was very pretty and had a lot of boyfriends, so there was never a dull moment!

Also, her sister liked to write stories just like she did. Brigitta missed not seeing her sitting on the swing under the apple tree with her notebook and pencil.

It was also an adjustment getting used to being in a large school with so many other students and teachers. Everything and everyone seemed to be so busy and rushed. She missed the camaraderie of her grammar school friends.

The wooden pine floors of the old junior high creaked as students crowded the hallways. The building was always stuffy and hot. Opening the windows did not help that much.

Snacks were not allowed in the classrooms. Brigitta and her classmates had to hurry and wolf down the candy bars they kept hidden in their backpacks in the breaks between classes.

There was no cafeteria in the junior high, so lunches had to be brought in from home and eaten in the homeroom. Students had to study either in their homerooms or in the auditorium. No talking was allowed during study-hall time.

Chapter 3

Aunts, Uncles and Cousins

It was during this busy time of change that many of Brigitta's relatives were moving out of Pennsylvania and relocating to Michigan. Brigitta's mother was very devoted to her sisters and brothers. It was hard for her to see them move so far away.

Religion was suddenly becoming a problem. Some of her aunts and uncles joined a religion requiring women to wear black stockings and coil their hair in a bun rather than having it curled. They also had to wear simple plain clothing. Jewelry and make-up were forbidden.

They would no longer be exchanging Christmas gifts or even have a tree for the holidays. Movies and dance were forbidden. It all sounded very strange and strict. But Brigitta's parents felt really bad when they were told that "unless they joined this new religion, they were no longer welcome in their home and most certainly would not go to heaven!"

It was not a happy time. Brigitta's parents had a hard time understanding why all this was happening. It seemed that their world of visiting with family and enjoying picnics together was being turned upside down.

Brigitta heard her parents discussing this new situation and wondering what to do. She hoped her parents would not join this religion because if they did, then she would have to give up going to dancing school! Why, she wondered, would people want to be so austere? If music and dance were forbidden, then would the birds have to stop their happy singing? And what about all those beautiful flowers in the fields and meadows? Would Mother Nature have to cover them up?

None of it seemed to make sense. Brigitta felt sad for her parents since they were caught up in the middle of a problem they didn't know how to solve.

But the worst part of everything was the fact that the aunts, uncles, and cousins were moving to Michigan which seemed very far away. It was all due to the fact that job markets were changing. Coal mines were closing and brick yards were beginning to lay off workers. Many people lost their jobs.

About this time things were changing in the railroad industry as well. There was talk of replacing steam engines with diesel fuel. Big trucks were starting to transport more goods, meaning that fewer jobs would be available in the railroad industry. Most of the men in Brigitta's family had been working in coal mines. With the closure of many mines, fewer freight trains would be needed to haul coal here and there.

Already, Brigitta had noticed that there were fewer trains along the crossroads in the East End area along the Susquehanna River than there were a year ago. Although the big black puffing steam engines had seemed so scary, she missed seeing them. Things were changing all over much too fast.

One of the uncles and aunts who moved to Michigan used to rent the CCC cabins in the Black Moshannon State Park every summer. When they moved, that meant the end of family picnics in that beautiful park of honeysuckle and pink mountain laurel blossoms. There would no longer be family gatherings and walks along the huckleberry trails along the river. The park was such a beautiful place to spend a Sunday afternoon and Brigitta knew she and her family would miss the gatherings that would no longer take place.

Although the waters in Black Moshannon State Park were brown from the marshy sediment, swimming still felt good and refreshing. The park was not far from her grandmother's house and the old German cemetery where some of their relatives on her mother's side were buried.

Brigitta thought of the years when she was little and they had stopped at Whispering Pines, a small park where they could picnic and swing on the swings while on their way to Black Moshannon State Park. Now that would be changed forever. It didn't seem fair.

Fortunately, Brigitta's Uncle Alfred still lived in the Revloc, Pennsylvania area. This meant she and her parents would have some family to visit even though driving to Revloc, a coal mining town, meant having to smell the huge coal bony-pile that was always burning and smelled terrible! The bony-pile was left-over shale from the coal mining strippings and could be smelled for miles and miles.

Uncle Alfred lived in one of the company houses owned by the coal company. The company houses were two-story houses that all looked alike.

The town of Revloc was at least a two-hour drive away. Brigitta's father did not like to drive that far. Sunday was his day to rest after working in the mines. Driving there meant being gone for a whole day.

Next to move were her Aunt Martha and Uncle Bill, her favorite aunt and uncle who lived in Coalport. They had decided to move to Lansing, Michigan to join other relatives who had already moved. This meant the end of Sunday road trips up and over the hills to that sleepy little town. They could no longer spend Sundays with some of Brigitta's favorite aunts and uncles.

Chapter 4

Activities

Brigitta's parents weren't much for joining church, although they visited various ones from time to time. The one that Brigitta liked best was the little country Shawville Methodist church tucked in the mountains and reached by a winding road just off the main highway.

She sometimes found it boring, though, when members started praying out loud. One person would start to pray, then another one followed, and soon every member in the congregation would say "amen" followed by a chorus of amens. It seemed to go on forever.

When she was younger, Brigitta had participated in the summer children's programs. That meant memorizing long verses of poems and reciting them to the entire congregation. One year she was one of many children who marched around the pews singing "Onward Christian Soldiers." That was a special day as the whole church was decorated with wild pink roses that grew along the mountainsides. It was one of her fondest memories.

As she grew older, she joined the church's youth fellowship group. They met in each other's houses, played games, and sang songs. Once in a while they met in a vacant shed along the highway close to the Shawville Methodist Church where they visited and shared this or that.

Sometimes they met at her house in the basement room that her parents had built with their own hands, using shovels and pitch forks when Brigitta was little. The room was built under her parents' bedroom and ended up being quite nice and roomy, with a door leading to the rest of the basement, as well as an outside door.

A big victrola/record player was set up so everyone could dance and listen to music. Brigitta's mother checked on them from time to time. She didn't know, however, that one of the games they sometimes played was "Spin the Bottle." Someone would spin the bottle and got to kiss whoever the bottle pointed to. It was quite fun and they had a lot of laughs as the kisses were quick and not everyone did it. If they wanted to do a dance or tell a joke instead, they could. Most of the boys chose the jokes or doing a funny dance.

All in all, it was harmless fun and they had a good time, especially since nearly all of them, like Brigitta, lived in an area with no close neighbors or friends, so it was extra special for the group to be able to meet together.

Chapter 5

Riding the Bus

Brigitta was happy that the school bus to the junior high and high school stopped at her mailbox on its way from the mountain. Now she didn't have to walk the mile to the gas station where she had taken the bus to the elementary school. The bus wasn't regular, time-wise, and once in a while when she missed it, she had to walk the nearly four miles or so to the junior high school.

One day when her bus was parked with a lot of other buses in front of the junior high, she got on the wrong one. She didn't know it was the wrong one as it had been a tiring day, and she fell asleep. She woke up just as the bus driver was getting ready to park his bus for the night in his garage. Just as she realized she was all alone, the bus driver saw her and said, "And where did YOU come from??" He wasn't happy that he had to drive the whole way back over the mountain to take her home. That made for a very long day for both of them.

Another time, when the bus stopped to let her off, she started walking across the road just as another bus came roaring around the corner to pass. She managed to dash out of the way as it screeched on its brakes to stop! Buses, it seemed, liked to dare each other to see who could get home the quickest and were always trying to see which one could get done with their run first. Not too long after that, a law was passed stating that buses and all other vehicles had to stop when a school bus was unloading passengers.

Brigitta also discovered that it was difficult to participate in some of the after-school activities. If she did, she had to find another way home which usually meant walking.

There were two different routes she could walk. One led up and down a hill and through two sleepy little villages called Sheep's Rock and Kerr Addition, both of which were along the north side of the road. The road was quite narrow, with not much room for walking. On the south side there was a steep embankment leading to the Susquehanna River. Brigitta had to be very careful when cars came speeding up or down the hill. She didn't want to end up falling into the river!

The second route led through downtown Clearfield, then up a steep mountain to a town called East End situated along the south side of the main highway. Most of the people who lived in East End were Italians and not many of them could speak English. The houses and stores were quite close together, with side streets all over the place.

A sprawling brick yard and a number of railroads were on the north side of the road along the Susquehanna River. Brigitta had to cross over the busy railroad tracks to get to the bridge over the river and then follow the road that led to her home. She had to hurry as sometimes homeless men lived in shacks along the riverbanks, so she had to be very watchful. One of the bridges that crossed the river was so old that the school bus had to stop and let its passengers walk across the bridge before it could cross.

The buses usually took the route through Kerr Addition, but if it rained for several days, the roads would flood over, and then the buses would have to take the route through East End. The schools would close if the weather caused too many problems.

Chapter 6

Girls and Boys

Despite the fact that boys and girls visited during youth fellowship classes at church or intermingled during school hours, they hadn't paid much attention to each other. They had all been busy just trying to adjust to life in junior high. But now things were changing.

During one of the bus rides to school, one of the boys who sat beside Brigitta laid his arm casually along the back of her seat. This was okay because he seemed rather "cool" in his junior high basketball shirt, but when his long fingers started moving down her shoulder, that was enough! She wasn't ready for a boy to be that familiar. A harmless kiss during a game of Spin the Bottle was one thing, but a wandering hand was quite different.

However, later on, when he offered to let her wear his junior varsity sweater, that was another matter. But that, too, didn't last long, since if wearing the sweater meant giving permission for hands to wander, then the sweater had to go back to its owner.

The year was going fast. Soon it was time for the junior high prom. Dance lessons were offered for boys and girls during gym class. One of her classmates, Ward, offered to take her to the prom. Brigitta wasn't sure whether to accept or not. Ward could be rather loud and boastful but he was someone she had known in elementary school and felt comfortable with him, even though one day back in sixth grade he had brought a mouse to school in his pocket! He was friendly and fun so she decided it would be all right to accept his offer.

What to wear? Brigitta poured through the Montgomery Ward Sales Catalog and ordered a turquoise blue chiffon dress with a white lacy collar. Next, she and her girlfriend, Ellen, went shoe shopping. They each bought a pair of brushed velvet black shoes with two-inch heels. Then they practiced walking in them, which they found out wasn't so easy! When the package with her dress came in the mail, she was quite excited. The dress looked really beautiful and it fit perfectly.

When the day of the prom arrived, her dad drove her and Ward to the junior high gymnasium where the prom was held. Brigitta felt quite grown up. It was quite the fun to see everyone dressed up, and it turned out to be quite the nice evening. Life was, indeed, getting interesting.

Chapter 7

4-H Strawberry Disaster

Ever since grade school Brigitta had been a member of a local 4-H club. She had always enjoyed 4-H and had learned skills such as how to make a bed, cook scrambled eggs, arrange flowers, and other skills. One summer she decided to grow strawberries through the 4-H extension program.

This was quite a job as it involved planting 375 plants and taking care of them. Her father grudgingly agreed to plow up a section of the field for her plants. It was no easy chore to keep them watered and weeded, but when the blossoms started coming on, it was quite rewarding. Usually, the first year of the strawberry plants involves plucking the blossoms so they will bare bigger and better fruit the next year.

Brigitta, however, could not wait. It seemed a waste not to let the blossoms bear fruit, plus with school ending and the dance recital to prepare for, there was little time to be plucking blossoms off so many plants. She let the berries ripen. Soon the whole patch was red with berries.

But, 375 plants meant a lot of strawberries and Brigitta realized she could not keep up with them. When she mentioned to her dancing school friends, the twins, about her problem, they offered to come over and help her pick them. Her father drove the ten miles to the little town where they lived and brought them over to her house.

After a visit and light lunch, the three of them headed off to the field. After they had been picking for an hour or more, Brigitta suddenly realized something was terribly wrong. The object was to pick berries, put them in quart baskets and sell them. The twins, however, were removing the caps from them before they put them in baskets. In other words, they were cleaning the berries as they picked them.

"Oh, no," said Brigitta in horror when she saw what they were doing. "We can't sell them if they are cleaned," she told them. Too late. By now the twins were tired of picking and ready to go home. Brigitta had a bunch of cleaned berries she didn't know what to do with and dreaded having to tell her father that she had neglected to instruct her friends the proper way to pick berries.

"Why didn't you show them how to do it?" scolded her father when she finally told him what happened.

In the end, Brigitta's mother made up several batches of strawberry jam. This was a good thing as everyone liked jam, but by not being able to sell what they picked, that meant they would not earn any money. That was the end of the big strawberry project as the next year her father decided the field would do better if he grew hay instead of strawberries.

Brigitta learned a big lesson: if you ask someone to help you with something, then be sure to give them instructions on how to do it!

The next summer when she visited the twins, they picked wild strawberries together in a field outside of their town. Wild strawberries are very small but much tastier than cultivated ones. They picked enough for strawberry shortcake as well as filling their own stomachs. Those were berries they could pick and enjoy, and on a warm summer day, there was no better treat.

Chapter 8

Gaining Confidence

Brigitta had been faithfully practicing toe/point ballet every chance she got on the linoleum floor in the living room. She also practiced diligently on the beautiful wooden pine floors at the dancing studio in downtown Clearfield. By now, she was becoming good enough at dance that she was asked to perform at school and different public functions.

She also had gained confidence with both public speaking as well as solo dancing. "Just pretend you are talking and/or dancing to a field of cabbages," a teacher told her. She discovered that although she would get flutters in her stomach, those flutters would disappear after a while. She just should never give up, she was told.

Her confidence in public speaking also came from the many recitations she had done along with other students in school and in church. She found out she loved to be on stage. Dancing and public speaking seemed to come naturally.

Maybe it was all those "cabbage" heads that had given her confidence!

Some of the clubs Brigitta joined in junior high included the Radio Club, which meant a class trip to Pittsburgh to visit the KDKA Radio Station. She also joined the archery club and enjoyed practicing archery with her new bow.

Her parents joined the Mt. Joy Grange organization. This was another place where Brigitta, as well as her parents, participated in many of their programs. She would dance or recite, her mother would play the piano, her dad would sing, and together they would do skits.

The Grange was an organization formed to help farmers and rural people, in general. There were several degrees one could earn if you wanted to. The degrees were earned through secret rituals which were both serious and fun. Brigitta and her parents earned six degrees throughout the years. Seventh degree was the highest one could obtain.

Grange offered a lot of interesting programs as well as wonderful potlucks. The farm women were good cooks so there were a lot of great pies, cakes, and main meals. At county fair time, each Grange had their own booth in the community building and each vied to be the best. The booths held all kinds of canned goods, cakes, pies, breads and cookies, as well as crafts, quilts, and such. Brigitta and her friend Ellen helped with setting everything up in the booth as well as taking it down when the county fair was over.

When not involved in other things, Brigitta poured through magazines and clipped articles about famous ballet dancers. Reading about them gave her encouragement to keep working hard on perfecting her own skill. While many of her friends were happily visiting other friends and having sleepovers, Brigitta was faithful with her dance practice.

Chapter 9

Trial and Error

Some things that Brigitta tried didn't work out. She watched the junior high band practice in the park across the street from the school and decided that looked like a lot of fun. Of course, this meant she would need to learn how to play an instrument and with that in mind she went to see the band teacher.

"Let's try the clarinet," said the band teacher as he opened a closet and pulled out a strange-looking slender musical instrument. He showed her how to use the reeds and how to take care of it.

After taking a number of lessons with the band teacher, she felt she was ready to try marching with the band. But this didn't quite work out as she had planned because she found out it was hard to read the music, find the right keys on the clarinet, and march at the same time. Maybe this wasn't for her.

She kept working at it for quite a while until she finally realized she was making squeaky music instead of good music. Regretfully, she returned the clarinet back to the music room closet. "I guess that's not for me," she woefully told the teacher. He just smiled.

Maybe orchestra would work out better. Brigitta remembered that her cousin had given her parents an old violin. Maybe she could learn to play it. With rosin for the bow, and sheets of simple music, she practiced, and practiced, and practiced.

Reading music was easy as in grade school everyone had been taught how to do it. At that time, she had learned to play the tonette, a small recorder.

Getting to orchestra practice at the junior high was another matter. She tried balancing the violin on the handlebars of her bicycle as she peddled the three miles to the high school for practice. That worked okay on fair weather days but not on rainy ones, not to mention that winter was coming on. Maybe playing violin wasn't a good idea, either. Maybe she should stick with dance and leave it at that.

The junior high school had a Minstrel Show every spring and asked for performers to volunteer. Brigitta auditioned, became a regular dance performer. and did many ballet solos. She also joined the girls' choir.

Through the years she and other dance students had idolized the older dancers that were so good. But now, through practice every night, she was becoming proficient on her toes and was asked to be the lead in their group ballets. Maybe she couldn't be in the marching band, but at least she could dance in the Minstrel Shows.

Chapter 10

Poetry and Problems

During these years Brigitta found out that poetry was something that she found easy to do. She started keeping journals of her poems and stories. Writing seemed to come naturally. When she was in grade school, she had written a newsletter and had sold it to her classmates for two cents each.

Her sister also was good at writing stories and had come up with "Lillian, the rabbit" stories. Brigitta and her sister would find a place in the woods or under the apple tree for writing stations. She also started keeping a diary. That was something her mother had helped her with in grade school. She tried to remember to write in it every day.

One day she decided to share her journals of poetry with her Junior High School English teacher. It was not easy to do so as her writings were personal and private. She was hoping for encouragement.

That was not what happened. Instead of encouragement, she was given a stern lesson on plagiarism. "What is plagiarism?" she asked her teacher. "Plagiarism," she was sternly told, "means copying the works of others," and her teacher named several women poets, one of which she told Brigitta her work resembled.

Brigitta quietly listened and closed her journals. She felt very embarrassed. She had never read the works of any of the poets her teacher had mentioned. She would never think of copying anyone else's stuff. Crestfallen, she decided she would not share her own work with anyone ever again.

That didn't stop her from writing, however, and she continued writing more than ever. Writing was as much a part of her as was dancing, something she just couldn't stop doing. She also loved to read, which was something her father loved to do, too.

Brigitta's mother played the piano when she had free time. She had never taken lessons and yet had mastered very difficult music. Her beautiful piano music would drift through the house, while in the evenings, her father sat reading in his big comfortable chair.

There wasn't a lot of free time for her mother as she was quite busy taking care of the cow, milking it and straining the milk, as well as feeding chickens and preserving foods. Every spring she wall-papered and/or painted the walls in the bedrooms, kitchen and bathroom. This had to be done because the coal dust from the furnace made the walls dirty.

The big floor-size radio was important in Brigitta's home, and offered a lot of programs that her mother enjoyed listening to while baking bread, frying donuts, or preparing meals. They could get stations from all over the world just by the turn of a knob. Sometimes the wiring in the back of the radio got loose and Brigitta would fix it.

Brigitta played records on the big victrola for dance practice. Some of the music included: *Valse Bluette* by Eugene Ormandy, *Coppelia Waltz* by Eugene Ormandy, *Music in Springtime, Springtime Ballet, Valse Trieste, Les Sylphides*. Also, music from the movie *Red Shoes*, starring Moira Shearer. Brigitta saw the movie three times.

Chapter 11

Going On

Seventh grade went all too fast. The summer flew by and now it was time for 8th grade. Brigitta's home room was on the second floor of the old junior high building. She was glad to be out of the 7th grade basement homeroom.

Classes included math, English, history, geography, home economics, health, music and gym. The history teacher was stern and gruff and not many students liked him, although Brigitta did. One of the things he talked about was the "Balance of Nature," the theory that "if and when the world becomes too populated, nature would create disasters such as earthquakes, tornadoes, flood or illness to keep the population under control." Brigitta did not know what to think about that!

Gym class was a challenge as Brigitta did not much care for sports, especially after a school softball game when a fast ball hit her friend in the eye and knocked her out. Her friend was all right, but the incident caused quite the alarm.

Math class was difficult. In 7th grade her teacher had been hard to understand and, somehow or other, Brigitta got lost with it all and never ever again was comfortable with mathematics.

In home economics class students learned how to sew an apron, cook and learn basic housekeeping. Brigitta had learned a lot of that through 4-H years earlier.

The class students seemed to appreciate the least was health. No one was comfortable with the talk of hygiene and/or sex education. Girls were separated from boys when it came to talks about their bodies. Boys and girls were also separated for movies on hygiene matters.

The movies that girls attended taught such things as "don't eat crackers in bed," be respectful to others, and good manners. Some of the movies were about marriage that advised such things as "don't yell at your husbands," and "be sure to wear nice apparel to bed." Brigitta thought it was a waste of time. Manners, she thought, should be taught by one's parents. But, of course, not everyone had good parents.

While in dancing school, Brigitta and her friends, the twins, already had studied quite a bit of sex education. They did it secretly so their parents wouldn't know. Their method was when one of them would hear of a word they didn't understand, they would take turns looking it up in a dictionary. They would write it down and hide the information in their shoes so they could share their new knowledge with each other at their next dance lesson. A lot of the words were confusing and somewhat scary. They had a lot of laughs as they discussed things. But they felt pride in their new found knowledge.

Most of the girls planned to marry as soon as they graduated from high school or even before. To be a wife and mother was considered an esteemed role and one most of them were anxious to fulfill. If one chose the working world, the career options for women were not very good, other than teaching, being a nurse or a secretary.

Chapter 12

Travels and Downtown

When Brigitta was fourteen, her parents took her to Gettysburg to see the Civil War battlefield. The whole area had a sad and somber feel to it. She could almost feel the presence of the soldiers on both sides who had fought so hard for what they believed. She had always been interested in history, and the trip further inspired her to study it more. She felt sorry for the hundreds of Union and Confederate soldiers who had lost their lives.

That summer, Brigitta and her mother took several bus trips to Michigan to visit aunts and uncles who had relocated there from Pennsylvania. Her Aunt Martha lived in a very nice big brick house on a corner on Hillsdale Street in downtown Lansing.

All of her relatives who had moved to Michigan seemed happy. Many of them had had to work in the coal mines when in Pennsylvania. Her Uncle Bill had the beginning of lung disease from all the years of working underground in the wet, damp, confined coal mines.

Although Junior High School proved to be a busy time for Brigitta, she and her girlfriends found time in between school and dance class to explore downtown Clearfield. The two 5 & 10-cent stores on opposite ends of the main shopping street were interesting to explore, especially the one on the far end that had a basement that was full of bargains.

There were several soda shops that offered lemon-cherry-blend cokes, as well as milkshakes served in tall glasses along with tin containers that contained the overflow. One of the soda shops was on the first floor of a building that housed a dentist office on the second floor. Brigitta spent a lot of time at the dentist office as her teeth seemed to need a lot of fixing. The dentist would get out his drill and drill away. There was so much drilling that smoke poured out of the drill, Brigitta clutched the dentist chair as she tried hard to be brave and bear the pain. Finally, when drilling was done, the filling was put in the tooth.

After the tooth was filled, the dentist gave her money to buy a sundae in the soda shop downstairs. The dentist and her father were good friends. Maybe it wasn't a good idea to eat a sundae after getting a tooth filled, but it sure tasted good!

Clothing shops in downtown Clearfield included J. C. Penny's, and Brody's. The Brody's shop sold mostly expensive dresses but it was fun to go in and try them on. Brigitta liked their Ship and Shore blouses and once in a while had enough money to buy one with money she earned from baby-sitting.

Several hardware stores, furniture stores, Mom and Pop grocery stores, and the volunteer fire station were downtown along with the county courthouse.

Leitzinger's was a department store with a creaky black metal elevator operated by an elevator man that took them up to other floors. Their merchandise was a little too pricey for Brigitta and her family. At Christmastime, the third floor was converted into toyland. Leitzinger's had a unique method for processing money. After handing the clerk money, it was put it into a cylinder that was sent through special tubing up to the second floor where the payment was processed. Change would be sent back down the tube.

The many downtown stores included several shoe stores, hat stores, and jewelry shops. The beautiful tall Dimeling Hotel was on a main corner. A doorman stood at the entrance. On one of the walls in the hotel entrance on the first floor was a huge mural of buffalos. The hotel had a coffee shop and a large ballroom where performances and/or dances were held. Brigitta went there sometimes as a member of the school's girls' chorus to give special performances.

There were three movie theatres downtown: the Lyric, that showed mostly westerns; the Roxie that showed whatever the other theatres did not show, and the Ritz that showed the newest and best-rated movies. The Ritz was right alongside the dancing school. If there was time, Brigitta went to the movies in between dance classes on Saturdays. Movies were twenty-five cents, the same price as a marshmallow sundae in the Ritz Restaurant beside the movie theatre. Sometimes it was hard to decide whether to spend her money on the movie or the sundae!

Chapter 13

Cliches and Clubs

Brigitta soon discovered that in junior high school some students formed little cliques or groups for sleepovers and such. She could not be a part of any of them since she lived so far out of town. No matter, she was aspiring to be a ballerina.

There were a lot of opportunities to use her dancing skill. The six years of lessons and almost daily practice much improved her dancing skill and she was invited to perform at various places. One of the solo ballet dances she did while in junior high included dancing to the Coppelia Waltz by Eugene Ormandy in the 7th Grade Minstrel Show. She also danced in the local hospital, the local Granges, and the Dimeling Hotel.

Other events included going with the school dance band, and with other solo vocal and musical performers, to perform in small towns such as Bellefonte and Phillipsburg.

It was a great honor to participate with other dance members in doing a solo dance in the Kiwanis Capers music production that performed in DuBois and in Clearfield. The beautiful main performer was a special guest artist from Austria.

Sometimes Brigitta would spend the night with another student who lived in town so they could leave the next day to go together and drive to the town where they would perform.

At one of the places where she danced, the dance floor was so slippery that she fell. No problem, as she quickly got up and resumed the dance. That's what one had to do, just keep on going no matter what. That was one of the pitfalls of performing on a regular dance floor instead of a stage. Dance floors tended to be slippery.

A rumor circulated in dance school that one of the students, Ivadeen, had moved to New York City with her mother to audition for the New York City Rockettes dance group. Sure enough, they heard later that Ivadeen had been successful with her audition and was now a member. That gave everyone something to think about.

Brigitta carefully tucked the lamb's wool into her toe shoes and practiced harder. She dreamed of going to the Julliard School of Music to further her dance, and yet she knew that was mostly a dream. Money was tight in her family these days as her father's work was not as regular as it had been. Brigitta heard her parents discussing what to do and how they could cope.

Workers were being laid off from jobs all over town. Even the brick yards were starting to lay off workers. The times were becoming tough. Many families were starting to move away.

Chapter 14

Uncertainty

Although Brigitta's father was a hard worker, he wasn't able to keep a steady job for long. Every company he worked for, it seemed, would start laying off workers and he would be one of the ones laid off. Some of the companies closed permanently.

Brigitta's father was a coal miner not because he wanted to be but because there weren't any other jobs available. He tried owning his own coal mine and leased some property for that purpose for a while, but that didn't work either. He started taking a course through the mail to be a Mining Inspector but with the mines closing everywhere there would be no need for inspectors. "Maybe," Brigitta heard her father tell her mother, "I should start going to other cities and see if I can find work." Maybe it was time for them to move somewhere else.

"Other cities?" That didn't sound good, thought Brigitta. She loved her father and hated to think of him having to go away. What would they do? Would they have to move? How awful!

Her mother had never learned to drive a car as they had only one, and her father used it for driving to work every day. When he went to another town for work, he would take the bus and leave the car at home. With him gone, her mother would need to drive, so she started taking driving lessons. It wasn't easy for her and it took a while. She failed a couple of the driving tests, but finally succeeded. There were few jobs available for women, but she found one at a laundrymat in downtown Clearfield.

Brigitta hated to see her mother going off to work outside the home. Her father didn't like it either as he had always said that "no woman of mine will work outside the home as long as I can help it." But now, he couldn't as they needed the money and he would be far away.

Brigitta decided that perhaps she could help somehow, too. That summer she and her girlfriend Ellen took a job picking berries on a strawberry farm on top of one of the mountains in the Wolf Run area. The strawberry owner kept the outside radio on for them to listen to while they were picking berries. It was on June 25, 1950, while they were picking berries that they heard on the radio that shots had been fired in a faraway place called Korea, and that might be the beginning of a war.

Brigitta had no idea where Korea was until she looked it up on a map. She dreaded to think of another war since it did not seem so long ago that World War II had ended. The idea of another war somewhere in the world, did not sound good.

Strawberry picking lasted only until the season was over, which it was in another week. She would have to think of something else to do to earn money.

Chapter 15

Ninth Grade and Beyond

Brigitta had many dreams of what the future might hold. She was hoping that somehow or other she could go to college and become a teacher. But her father had other ideas, and when it was time to choose what courses to take in high school, she knew her dream of being a teacher would not be possible.

To go to college to be a teacher, she would need to take the college preparatory course. The two other choices available were commercial and general. When she sat down to discuss things with her parents, her father was adamant that she enroll in the commercial course. There was no money for college he said, and by taking the commercial course she would not have to attend business school as her sister had to do, plus, she would be able to find a job right away.

Brigitta was not happy with enrolling in the commercial courses, but she had to follow her father's wishes. One of the subjects in the ninth grade was General Business Training. It was hard to get interested and study for a class that seemed to be so boring. Numbers and math were difficult subjects for her and her attention waned.

She never liked taking tests, either, and had difficulty with them.

Her mind, it seemed, just couldn't concentrate on pulling certain information out of a greater portion. The things she studied for were never on the tests or exams.

Test questions involved some things that she hadn't considered important and hadn't memorized them. She still managed to pass them but not with a high score. Fortunately, because her grade average was high, she was exempt from most exams.

Music and art were the subjects she mastered but she knew she couldn't make a living or get a job in either of those areas. At least not without a college degree. Reluctantly, she signed up for the commercial courses.

❧ ⊙ ☙

Chapter 16

❧ ⊙ ☙

Things Unexpected

By now, her sister Mary had finished her legal secretarial training at business school and was working in a lawyer's office. When Mary was away at school, she remembered to send special gifts to Brigitta for her January birthday. She always included valentine candy with her gifts.

But the nicest gift that Mary gave to Brigitta was a soft light blue corduroy vest with sequins along the front and a beautiful matching blue corduroy skirt. Brigitta had been admiring the outfit in a clothing store window but knew she could never afford it. She was surprised to open the package and see such a beautiful outfit, and when she wore it, she felt like a princess.

The summer went all too quickly. Brigitta spent it writing as well as practicing ballet. She loved to hike the Big Hill in back of her house and sit with a good book and a notebook and pencil and listen to the whippoorwill. She loved to watch the clouds and all their formations, and loved sitting among the pink wild roses that bloomed all over the hill.

One of the highlights of that summer was going to Atlantic City, New Jersey, to take the Seventh Degree, the highest degree offered by the Grange.

The Mt. Joy Grange decided to participate in the trip and to travel by bus to the Madison Hotel in Atlantic City. Brigitta's girlfriend, Ellen, went along, as she, too, was interested in the Grange. The day after they settled in the hotel, they took the initiation for the Seventh Degree. They had now earned the highest degree that a Grange member could earn.

That same summer, Brigitta and Ellen picked strawberries again for the farmer on the hill above the Susquehanna River for the last time.

There was a big party that summer for Otis Fulton, a bachelor teacher, who had just married. He lived in a beautiful two-story big house with a wrap-around porch on the mountain overlooking the railroad tunnel and Susquehanna River. Everyone in the area attended that wonderful event.

Soon it was time for the County Fair. Brigitta, her friend Ellen, along with her cousin Carol, helped to set up and take down the Grange display at the Fair. They were especially happy to do it as one of Ellen's sisters agreed to bake a chocolate cake to enter in the display. They were hoping the cake would still be edible by the time they had to take down the display.

"Let's go swimming afterwards," suggested Ellen. That seemed like a good idea because the weather was really hot. After they took down the display, they packed the cake, other goodies and their bathing suits, and headed for the swimming hole down in the mountains in the mountain creek. The area they were going to was many miles away but it felt good walking over the mountains and through the beautiful forests.

When they got to the swimming hole, they discovered to their dismay that they weren't the only ones there. Three high school boys were already in the water. The girls weren't sure what to do. Go or stay? They started a conversation with each other while playfully tossing stones in the cold little creek that was dammed up by rocks.

Finally, the girls took turns shielding each other behind pink blossoming laurel bushes so they could change into their bathing suits. This was the start of a whole new thought and adventure. The boys seemed friendly and harmless. They enjoyed visiting with one another as they splashed in the cold mountain water.

When it was time to go home, one of the boys offered to drive them back rather than let them walk. They took the offer. None of the girls had ever ridden in a car with boys their own age before. This was a whole new experience.

Chapter 17

Another Year and an Epidemic

Brigitta and Ellen both felt it was time they found employment to help out with home expenses so they wouldn't strain their families' incomes. One of Ellen's sisters worked at the area hospital. Maybe they could find a job there since they were now both fourteen. They went for an interview and were hired to work in the diet kitchen for 40 cents an hour.

It was a hot summer and the only way Brigitta could get to the hospital was to walk the four miles. This meant walking along the Susquehanna River and through the town of Kerr Addition. Brigitta didn't mind the long walk as she liked the work and felt important doing it.

But a sadness occurred at this time for suddenly an epidemic of polio swept throughout the community. Polio was a disease that health officials did not know how to handle. Arms and legs would become paralyzed and victims would not be able to walk. Some patients were put in an iron lung, a large tubular tank into which oxygen would be pumped to assist polio victims with breathing. Even with use of the lung many victims became paralyzed and/or died.

One day Brigitta heard that Hazel, a friend from Grange, had the disease. This was distressing news, especially since they had both just spent the night together on Hazel's beautiful farm in Mt. Joy. Hazel was in the hospital for a long time. Grange members donated money to help her parents cope with this tragedy. A new dress was sent to Hazel in hopes she would soon come home from the hospital. But, alas, although Hazel would be coming home, she would be paralyzed for life, never again regaining control of her legs. She would have to remain in a wheelchair the rest of her life.

At school more terrible news was heard when one of her classmates, Joey, contracted polio and had died. Joey had played the tuba in the marching band. Everyone was quite saddened as well as worried.

That fall, Brigitta's English teacher called her in to her office and talked to her about her job at the hospital. She knew that Brigitta was walking home from work. "This is not a good time to be walking so far when it is so hot and there is an epidemic of polio going on," she said. She told Brigitta that it would be best, in order to avoid the risk of getting tired and stressed and maybe come down with the disease, she should quit her job.

Reluctantly, Brigitta agreed to do just that, especially when she heard that her classmate, Joey, had died from the disease and that Hazel was now paralyzed.

Brigitta thought about an earlier disease called tuberculosis or TB. Her beautiful Aunt Esther, at age 28, had died from that disease just a few years before. There was, it seemed, always some kind of disease or war that people had to worry about.

She felt sad about having to quit her job at the hospital, but in a way that was okay since she had to walk home four miles and winter was on its way. There was no way she would be able to walk all that way during the winter. But now she had to think of another way to earn money.

Chapter 18

High School Challenge

Another year had passed and it was time to enter the two-story high school for a whole new adventure. The school was right across the street from the old junior high. It was a relief to be out of that rickety old wooden junior high building. Brigitta was relieved to be out of it since it had seemed like a fire trap with its wooden walls and creaky wooden floors.

Brigitta discovered that she didn't mind some of the commercial classes after all, and that she really enjoyed the typing class. Although she had planned to enroll in the German language class, she found that it had been replaced by Spanish due to World War II. No one wanted anything to do with anything German since that war had been started by Germany. Her parents had not taught her German for that same reason, although they spoke both German and English while at home. They felt it would be better for her not to learn German.

Along with her busy school schedule, Brigitta still attended dance school as well as many school and outside activities. Much of that involved performing solo ballet dances here and there. She loved every minute of it. Some days she would walk downtown Clearfield and pretend she was a famous ballet dancer, but, of course, she wasn't. But it was fun to dream.

She and Ellen went to Grange meetings as usual and enjoyed the comradeship of their various activities. After one meeting one of the older Grange members offered to drive them home. But when they got to Brigitta's house, they were startled when he wanted to kiss them. "Oh no!" they thought as they hurried out of the car. Growing up, they discovered, had its challenges!

POLKA PARTY
Presented by the Pupils of
Bette Y. Wellington School of Dancing
LYRIC THEATRE, CLEARFIELD, PA.
Monday, June 4, 1951

Fall Registration Satuday, September 22, 1951 at the Ritz Lodge Hall, from 2:00 to 7:00 P. M.

Part I

1. The Polka Party—Entire Cast.
2. The Dark Town Cane Strutters-?-?-?-?-?-?-?
3. It's The Rhythm— Sandy Brown.
4. Limber Lady Mona Lou Davis.
5. Five Dancing Dolls— Mary Ann Malloy, Barbara Cowdrick, Ivadeen Murray, Violet Jury, Nancy Reed.
6. The Dearie Girls—Barbara Bloom, Patty Jay, Marlyn Tibbins.
7. Acrobatic Miss— Peggy Jo Knepp.
8. Lovely Lady—Inge Logenburg.
9. Demure and Sweet— Betsy Anderson, Betsy Nolan.
10. Struttin—Sandy Brown, Mona Davis, Peggy Jo Knepp.
11. Acrobaticapers—Carol Duncan, Lyn Liddle, Kay Bartell, Betty Lou Cowdrick, Barbara Cowdrick, Judy Duckett.
12. On Her Toes—Kathleen Witherow.
13. Hoppin Down The Bunny Trail—Jo 'Ann Nemeth, Gail Nemeth, Janice Wilson, Gail Swisher, Gail Waroquier, Terry Cutler, Timmie Knepp.

Part II

1. Beautiful Ohio—Judy Brozgal, Phyllis Green, Barbara Bloom, Joyce Salvatore, Betty Lou Cowdrick, Sally Aughinbauch, Patty Aughinbauch, Susin Mullen, Nancy Reed, Betsy Anderson, Ivadeen Murray, Violet Jury, Betsy Nolan, Barbara Cowdrick, Mary Ann Malloy, Carol Duncan, Joan Mayersky, Kathleen Witherow, Peggy Jo Knepp, Mona Davis, Sandy Brown, Peggy Ann Lumadue, Inge Logenburg.
2. Neat and Nifty—Kathryn Johnson.
3. Acrobatix—Marlyn Tibbins.
4. Ballerina Dolls—Mona Davis, Sandy Brown, Peggy Jo Knepp.
5. Tuneful Taps— Ann Olmes, Mary Lou Thompson, Irene Learish, Betty Lou Cowdrick, Peggy Jo Czarnecki, Penny Knepp, Violet Jury, Carol Jean Kupko, Barbara Cowdrick.
6. Down On The Farm—Helen Adams, Patty Carns, Ann Bartley, Peggy Ann Lumadue, Mary Ann Malloy.
7. Starlettes— Peggy Jo Knepp, Mona Lou Davis.
8 San Souci Polka—Joan Mayersky, Carol Duncan.
9. Blue Danube Waltz—Susan Mullen, Patty Aughinbauch, Sally Aughinbauch, Betty Lou Cowdrick, Joice Salvatire, Barbara Bloom, Judy Brozgal.
10. Frosty The Snow Men and Ladies—Marlyn Tibbins, Patty Jay, Barbara Bloom, Ivadeen Murray, Helen Adams, Patty Carns, Ann Bartley, Peggy Lumadue, Eileen, Schenck, Clara Leitzinger, Mary Ann Malloy, Peggy Jo Knepp, Mona Davis, Sandy Brown.
11. The Tango—Kathryn Johnson.
12. Music In Springtime—Peggy Ann Lumadue.
13. Three Fancy Free Sailors—Peggy Jo Knepp, Sandy Brown, Mona Davis.
14. Three Tapsters—Clara Leitzinger, Eileen Schenck, Ivadeen Murray.
15. Under The Double Eagle March—Entire Cast.

THANK YOU

I take this opportunity to express my sincere thanks and gratitude to the parents and children who have worked with me during the past season to make our recital a success. To the many friends who come every year to encourage the children to entertain. We trust our presentation of 1951 will remain with you as a pleasant memory.

BETTE Y. WELLINGTON.

Brigitta's father was working out of town now. The house seemed very lonely and empty without him. He was trying out jobs in different towns and took a job in Cleveland, Ohio. That summer Brigitta and her girlfriend Ellen decided to take the bus and visit him.

Brigitta now had a little spending money as with her new typing skills she was asked to type insurance policies for one of the Grange members who was an insurance agent. She received twenty-five cents for each policy she typed. The office was upstairs over a clothing store in downtown Clearfield. The furniture and the cupboards were all beautiful oak. Two stained glass windows were above a desk. It was a pleasant office to work in. The money she earned added up quickly, and soon she had enough for a trip to visit her father in Cleveland. She and her girlfriend Ellen decided to go by bus.

Once they got to Cleveland, they booked a room in the same hotel where her father was staying. Brigitta thought he looked sad and she felt so sorry for him. Why did such things have to happen, that families had to be separated!

Her father wanted to show them the sights. They boarded the city bus. One of the things he was excited to do was to show them Euclid Beach along Lake Erie where they could go for a swim, but when they got there a big sign reading "Beach Closed. Waters Polluted" greeted them. Brigitta's father was very disappointed, as they were, too. Sadly, they returned to the hotel to sit and visit in the lobby.

Im between visiting with her father, they were able to visit some of the downtown stores. One, in particular, a women's clothing store, had a rich perfume aroma that they smelled as soon as they walked in. The clothes were beautiful and very expensive. It all seemed very exotic.

The bathroom in the hotel had nice towels and hot showers. When the girls left to go home, they packed a couple of the towels in their suitcase.

After they got home, they didn't feel right about doing that and threw the towels away.

Sometimes, Brigitta thought to herself, people do bad things and don't realize it's bad until too late. That was a stern lesson! She was finding out how life can be complicating and that it is a hard thing to avoid not getting caught up in the moment!

ॐ ☙
Chapter 19
ॐ ☙

The Driving Lesson

Since Brigitta's father was working out of town and her mother had a part-time job, it was important that Brigitta should learn how to drive. The driving lessons involved driving across the Susquehanna Bridge to one of the lumber yards. During one of the lessons when she turned the wheel, she started going around in circles and couldn't stop until her instructor grabbed the wheel and stopped the car! But after that she gained more confidence, and finally had enough courage to finish the lessons and take the driving test.

Everyone who took the driving test had to drive through the town area called East End, go up a steep hill, stop at the top, and then continue driving down the hill. Stopping at the top of the hill was the challenge that everyone dreaded. How do you stop a car, shift gears and manage to go forward without the vehicle slipping back down? Of course, because Pennsylvania had so many hills and mountains, it was very important to be good at shifting gears in tight situations.

When Brigitta got to the top of the hill, she started to break out in a sweat. Could she do it? Trying to remain calm and collected, she put her foot on the clutch and shifted into neutral. Using her foot on the clutch and brake, she had to be careful releasing both so that she didn't suddenly lunge forward or slide backward! Once she shifted out of neutral into low gear, she lifted her foot from the clutch and pressed down on the gas pedal. Whew! The car went forward smoothly. She had passed the most challenging part of the driving exam.

But when her driving teacher went with her to apply for her license, there was a problem. She failed the eye exam. This meant a trip to the eye doctor to be fitted for glasses. Once that was done, she could obtain the coveted driver's license. However, she certainly couldn't dance while wearing glasses, could she? Was this the end of her dream of being a ballerina? She wondered about that.

During these years Brigitta and Ellen had both started seeing and going out with two of the boys they had met at the swimming hole the summer before. Going out, or dating, meant visits to the local ice cream dairies, going for long walks, driving out in the evenings to spot deer in the mountains, or going to the drive-in theatre. She still stayed busy with school and dancing activities, but time was also spent with Ellen and the boys.

Brigitta and Ellen enjoyed their growing up years together. They both enjoyed having boyfriends. They went Christmas shopping together and explored the stores while trying to decide what would be the perfect gifts for these new friends. One time they both chose soft corduroy shirts for them. Another time they chose neat looking cigarette lighters that were boxed in satiny boxes.

Ellen did a lot of babysitting in the evenings, and when the family gave them permission, Brigitta, as well as the boys, would visit her. Together they would play with the children and fix special treats such as popcorn or strawberry shortcake.

Chapter 20

World Fears and Consequences

It was during Brigitta's junior year in high school when she started hearing rumors that were unsettling, that some of her girlfriends were leaving school to get married. It didn't seem possible, but when a schoolmate didn't appear in school for a few days, everyone realized that she had no intention of returning.

What was happening, Brigitta wondered and yet as she listened to the rumors that were floating throughout the rooms and halls, it seemed that world affairs were affecting some of her friends. Ever since the Soviet Union had detonated an atomic bomb as a test, people were getting scared. After World War II ended, there was dissension among several countries, and that the atomic bomb was something to be feared and dreaded.

It was during this time that some people started thinking of building underground shelters for protection. "If a bomb is going to drop and destroy things," said at least one girlfriend, "then we may as well get married now and have happiness while we can." Brigitta didn't know what to think about that.

Quitting school to get married seemed like a desperate thing to do, and yet several girlfriends did just that.

Pretty soon Linda quit school, followed by Patty and Jean. Brigitta didn't even have a chance to say goodby to them. One minute they were in school, and the next minute they were gone. Several boys left, also, to become husbands or to move off to another state for a job or adventure.

Brigitta and her friend Ellen double-dated several times with their boyfriends, but neither of them felt they were ready to drop out of school. There was a lot of studying yet to do, plus that high school diploma seemed to be very important. They had gone this far, they reasoned, and may as well continue.

Brigitta's sister Mary, insisted that she didn't intend to marry until she was thirty!

It was a time of exploring relationships, and of doing things together. Brigitta and her boyfriend spent some evenings at his grandfather's farm where they could sit close to the nice warm floor furnace register and drink cocoa. The farm was on the side of a mountain, fringed by a forest of tall pine and hemlock. Sometimes they went for walks through the woods or fields.

At night time they would drive out to the country to "spot" deer. This involved using a flashlight to see how many deer they could find in the woods and fields along the winding dirt country roads.

One rainy night after attending a movie to see *Titanic*, staring Barbara Stanwyck and Clifton Webb, Brigitta and her boyfriend decided to take a short cut through a dirt road when suddenly their car started sliding in the mud. Before they knew it, the car was leaning over a bank of a rushing mountain creek!

When her boyfriend decided to go and get help, Brigitta managed to climb carefully out of the car to go with him. However, she was wearing her new black velvety shoes and knew they would be ruined. But there was no way she was going to stay in the car by herself on a cold dark rainy night, plus it was possible that it could topple into the creek!

They both walked in the mud down the dirt road until they found a farmer who agreed to drive his tractor out to help them get unstuck. It was very late by the time Brigitta got home, and her father was not too happy!

Chapter 21

Disappointment and Tragedy

A big event for graduating seniors was a trip to Washington D.C. Brigitta's boyfriend, however, was unable to go. Neither he or his family could afford to pay for such a trip.

As if that wasn't disappointing enough, something happened that changed his life entirely. He was enrolled in the carpentry class in the vocational school and suddenly was injured using a radial saw machine while building a desk for his senior project. The saw did not have a safety guard on it, and his injury was so severe that he had to have immediate surgery. His hand was heavily damaged which meant he had to be very careful with what he did for quite a while until he was completely healed.

Being a senior, he was scheduled for a job in a lumber company but with his injury would not be able to do it. Another classmate was hired, instead. This was a big disappointment. Despite the injury, he was still able to work at the gas station where he had been working for a couple of years. He also managed to complete the very large desk that he had been working on in Carpentry Class as his senior project.

Brigitta went with his mother and sister to his Baccalaureate and Commencement. What would the future hold now?

Chapter 22

Tough Times

Life, thought Brigitta, poses a lot of challenges now and then. Everything around them seemed to be changing all too fast. Right after her father lost his job and had to seek a job in the city, everything started being different.

One of the changes involved strip mining. Now that the mines where her father had worked were closed, a new type of mining, strip mining, was starting to happen all over Pennsylvania. The mines where her father had worked were mostly underground. Miners dug tunnels and worked underground to find coal which everyone was using for their furnaces and factories.

Strip mining meant using heavy equipment to bulldoze and dynamite mountaintops. Heavy machinery would bulldoze woodlands of tall towering fir trees, creating a wasteland of stacked up trees and piles of dirt and deep holes. Miners would no longer do hand digging underground in tunnels. One day, just as her father was getting ready to go out of town for work, a group of men visited and told him that he would be paid a certain amount of money for each truckload of coal taken from the property.

It turned out that when her parents had bought their property years ago, they did not realize that the mineral rights, which meant whatever coal or anything else, that was on their property did not belong to them but belonged to the seller. The seller had the right to mine whatever mineral was on the property whether the owner liked it or not.

In other words, people had no choice but to let the big trucks come to bulldoze and tear up the mountains. It was a terrible time! When the trucks started roaring across the field and over to the mountain where Brigitta used to go sled riding, she knew nothing would ever be the same again.

The people who had lived on the mountain behind them had already moved away for the same reason. Brigitta wondered where they had moved to, and thought about the days when she was younger and had gone over there to watch the family make apple cider and to play with Peggy, a girl her own age.

She also remembered the days when Peggy used to come over to play paper dolls with her. Now she was gone.

Where did people go when they moved away? But things all over had been changing quietly all over the countryside. The big farmhouse that was along the main road across from them was being torn down. No longer were there black and white cows peacefully feeding in the meadowland across from their house. Farms all over the countryside were being dismantled or destroyed as soon as the strip-mining companies arrived.

The strip-mining companies moved in with their bulldozers, cranes and dynamite, and ripped everything up, destroying forests and farmlands, leaving large open holes or pits in the ground that quickly filled up with water. The companies left the holes and piles of dirt, and then moved on to strip elsewhere.

The big water holes that were left were very deep and sometimes people would go swimming in them and drown. In the wintertime the water would freeze over and be perfect places for ice skating. Brigitta, her sister, and a boy who lived on the other side of the mountain would go over to the next mountain to ice skate on one of the frozen holes even though it was a dangerous thing to do.

Strip-mining ruined many beautiful patches of wild huckleberries, sweet fragrant wild roses, pink and white mountain laurel, and towering pine forests. Brigitta wondered if the whippoorwill had to leave also. She didn't hear it any more so maybe they found other places to live. What about the bear and the deer? Where did they go? She wondered all of those things and felt very sad that everything so beautiful would have to be ruined.

Brigitta's father worried that the water supply from their mountain cistern would be gone. If so, they would no longer have running water for their household needs. The coal company told them that those things would be unharmed, but everyone had a bad feeling about everything. It wasn't long before Wolf Run, the sparkling little clean creek that ran by their house soon became tainted by orange runoff from the mines. Gone were the tadpoles, frogs and little fish. It was no longer safe to swim in. Brigitta's family hated what was happening to their little valley paradise, but there was nothing they could do about it.

Brigitta started writing stories about life and all the changes. She was glad that she had a boyfriend who came and helped with taking care of things now that her father was not around. It was up to her, her mother and sister to keep shoveling coal in the big furnace that heated their house and to put coal in the little stove in the basement so they could have hot water every day.

When heavy rains came and water flowed over the creek onto their yards and sometimes over the road, they had to deal with all of that. One by one, they started selling and giving away their animals, the cow and chickens, although Johnny, the goat, was still around.

Johnny scared them sometimes as he was a big goat. Sometimes he jumped up on the front porch and wouldn't let them go out the door. It seemed that there was trouble everywhere. Nothing, it seemed, would ever be the same again.

Chapter 23

Happiness is where you find it!

There still was a lot to be thankful for. Brigitta had a little Pomeranian dog, Topsy, that kept her company. Topsy was apricot in color and was playful and bouncy. One of their friends came and took Johnny, the goat. She was happy to see him gone.

Brigitta and her mother went to the movies when they found time. She and her boyfriend went to the movies, too. One of the movies they saw was "The House of Wax." It was a scary movie, and when she got home, a big storm came up with all kinds of loud thunder and lightning. That was a night that she didn't sleep very well as she was still scared from the movie, as well as the weather.

Her boyfriend was a year ahead of Brigitta in school and invited her to attend the senior prom. She bought a soft blue organdy dress from Brody's in downtown Clearfield. It was a special night to remember during a time of change and turmoil.

Brigitta still typed insurance policies once in a while for extra money and also picked strawberries again for Clyde Wilson, the strawberry farmer on the next mountain. There was very little money for anything. Her boyfriend gave a portion of the money he earned at a local service station to his parents. He also paid for the gas when his dad and sisters used the car. Brigitta used whatever money she earned to pay for dentist appointments, clothes, or gifts.

When it was time to order the yearbook, Brigitta's boyfriend paid for it.

Now that she was a junior in high school and the fact that there was no money remaining for dance lessons, she discontinued taking them. She still performed here and there, especially in the high school musical productions such as "Showboat" where she danced to Blue Rhapsody.

Brigitta kept busy in many ways. She stayed involved with the Future Teachers of America and helped as a teacher's aide in one of the elementary schools in downtown Clearfield and in high school she was still a member of the Future Nurses of America, the Radio Club, Girls Chorus, and, for a while, the Archery Club.

These were years of growing and learning. Also, a time of anticipation. Brigitta was sad that she and her parents would soon be moving away from the mountains she loved. They would be going to Michigan where her father had found a job with the automotive industry. She would be a senior in high school the next year and would be leaving her classmates and home of seventeen years. She knew it would not be easy going to a new school in her senior year.

A good thing about the move meant that she and her parents would, again, be close to relatives. Several aunts, uncles and cousins who had moved to Michigan several years ago, were eager to welcome them.

Moving meant new expectations and adventures. Wolf Run was no longer the quiet beautiful little valley that she had loved so much. She did not know what the future might hold. A career as a ballerina did not seem likely. Anyway, she had never seen a ballerina wearing glasses! But she knew that whatever she did, she would always have a love for dancing, and forever would dance in her heart.

It was a busy time packing and moving. It all happened so fast that Brigitta didn't have a chance to tell her school friends goodbye. They would never know why she moved and to where. She looked at her valley and thought of all the wonderful memories. She didn't know if she would like going to a city school for her senior year but, like it or not, it was time to move on. She would be with her parents whom she loved. That was all that mattered for now.

With Topsy in her arms, she looked back at the sad little house that now looked so empty. It had been a good life. It was a great place to grow up, but everything around them, was changing. She would miss the mountains and the morning misty fog but new adventures beckoned. She had packed all her journals that were full of stories and poems, and had an empty journal waiting for new stories. It was time to go.

Chapter 24

Mary's Remembrances

Mary remembers the Great Flood of 1936 and how she and her father walked to East End, and he hoisted her on his back so she could look over the mountain down into Clearfield and she saw water, water, water everywhere. Her friend Esther worked at Kurtz Brothers Papers and Supplies all her life until she retired. After the flood receded, Mary went with her parents to the Kurtz store and saw stacks and stacks of white ruled tablets on sale from water damage. The tablets all had blurry blue lines due to the flood.

Mary tells about a man who was staying in the downtown Dimeling Hotel and drowned in the flood. Some say he fell off a raft.

After the flood was over, the U.S. Army Corps of Engineers started work on building the Curwensville Dam and, eventually, the Curwensville Recreational Park.

A huge Walmart Store in Wolf Run, soon replaced a large stands of towering fir trees. Mary recalls walking through them with her mother and faithful dog, Fritzy. There was also an abandoned county road alongside of the bungalow her father built in Wolf Run. She and her mother walked it often.

When she was two or three, her parents drove to Florida, planning to live there; but once they arrived, they didn't like what they saw and drove back to Pennsylvania in their old Model T Ford automobile. They ended up renting rooms in one of three houses that stood at the edge of the hill in back of the current Alliance Church in Wolf Run. Mary loved living on the hill. She could look over the hill and across the Susquehanna River and see the old folks County Home and also the big tile factory. She felt like she was Queen of the Mountain!

Mary remembers relatives visiting them when they lived on the big hill and how "Rush" Stewart (she called him Grandpa Stewart) had a white beard and would sit on the porch in a rocker and watch her play. He was amazed that she washed a cat in a tub of water and it never complained! Mary loved living on the big hill and enjoyed playing with the neighbor children.

One cold blizzardy day in January, Mary was told to play outside a while. When she was told she could come back in, she was surprised to see her "mother looking very beautiful holding a beautiful little baby girl." The baby was her new sister, Brigitta.

She corrected Brigitta for telling people that Mary attended the one-room school in Wolf Run, saying that she had visited it only a couple times with Ruthie, who lived in the big white farmhouse across the field and meadow from the house Mary's father built in the valley in Wolf Run. She remembers the schoolhouse being built of logs of some sort.

When she did finally start first grade, Mary recalls running down the big hill to catch the bus and falling, thereby skinning her knees which then bled.

When her father bought some land down in the Wolf Run Valley, Mary was very upset. The valley seemed wet and dark. She recalls being depressed and upset with it all and "gave her parents a hard time." She did enjoy Wolf Run Creek that ran right beside their house and was delightful to swim and play in. That is until strip mining started in their area. Mineral sulphur water from the mining process ruined the little creek and turned it orange. (Many years later the creek still runs orange).

Also, the old Indian Mill that was along the creek beside the house was a great place to make mud pies, but in later years was buried with debris from hotels and motels that were built along the main road after Route 80 was constructed.

People were concerned, she remembers, that once Route 80 was built, there might be an increase in crime and drugs from people coming in from the eastern part of the country. Their fears were confirmed when the Wolf Run gas station's truck was stolen, although eventually found. Something like that had never happened before, until the completion of Route 80.

Mary's most painful memory, and one she had never shared until shortly before she passed, was when she was a young girl traveling back and forth from York, PA, to her Wolf Run home by train. Mary was a very beautiful blonde. It happened that one day she was very tired and maybe not thinking straight, as while she was on the train, a good-looking young man started a conversation with her.

He told her he was on his way to New York City to meet some friends and together they were going to see a special jazz group. Mary loved jazz and when he said he had extra tickets for the performance and would she like to go with him, she agreed. As they visited, he had some drinks and offered her some as well. He had this funny sort of laugh, a "he, he, he," which should have been a warning to her, as she thought about it later on.

When they reached New York, he took her to a hotel where he said they would meet with his friends. The hotel clerk wasn't ready to let them go upstairs to a room as they didn't have any baggage with them and there was a rule that "no baggage, then no room." Somehow or other he persuaded her that their luggage was on the way and she let them go. Mary followed him upstairs as she didn't want to wait alone in the hotel lobby.

Before they went in the room, she noticed that the room number was 149. After they entered his room, he immediately tried to call his friends to find out where they were but couldn't contact them. At that point, he suddenly made his move and tried to throw her on the bed. She screamed, remembering from movies that she had watched, that when women had a problem, they should grab something which they could used to swat their attacker! She quickly grabbed the bedside telephone with her free hand and called the operator. She told her she was being attacked in room 149.

The young man quickly grabbed his stuff and ran out of the room. A detective arrived, asked lots of questions, and said single girls should not be traveling alone. Then he helped Mary to get back on the train so she could get home. After that frightening incident she never wanted to go to New York City again. The morale of the story is: Never go any place with a stranger! Also, if she hadn't read the room number before they went in, things might not have turned out so well. She felt that surely a Guardian Angel was watching over her!

Mary did go to New York City many years later with her mother to take Tante Trudy to board a steamship to return to Germany. The captain of the steamship, at the time, was a brother-in-law from Europe.

Chapter 25

Odds and Ends

Following are some of the poems Brigitta wrote while in high school:

Our School Bus

Our school bus is yellow, has many nice fellows
It never does come on time (what else can rhyme?)
With other buses we race, each holding his place
Our bus is so merry (when it stops at the dairy)!
Our bus is quite jolly, and that is no folly
The kids can make noise (it's mostly the boys).
Our bus can go sixty, but the bus company says "nix-ty"
We swerve around cars (our windows have no bars)!
The kids know lots of songs. They mostly sing them wrong
But we always have fun, and worries none.

May

Daffodils yellow
no more fellow
blossoms
pink
become extinct

lilies white
fade night
violets blue
over, too.
May fleet
spring heat
passes by
time flies.

Junior High Band

Bugles sounding, breaks the lull
sends through the air commanding call
Piccolos calling, their tone sweet
trills and whistles down the street
loud message of drums rhythm and beat
drumstick twirling, busy feet.

Love

What everyone strives for, everyone's greatest need
is to be loved by someone, with lots of "love feed."
It's not to be played with, put aside with tears
but to be upheld, through all of life's years.
Love is protection, it hides human fears
Love is a great fondness, and holds moments dear
Love cannot be explained for words are too small.
Find someone who knows, to explain it all!

Evening

A mystic mysterious magic spell fills the cool silent evening
Pale clouds slowly move over the dim hazy blue
Gray barren trees stretch their limbs hungrily to the sky
Little violets daintily close their petals for the night
Tiny specks of green leaves illuminate themselves
against withered bark
From somewhere in the forest a lonely bird calls to its mate
Then all is quiet as night slowly approaches with her mystic
mysterious black cloak.

The Prom

Warm, fresh spring air, fragrant of violets, green grass and new rustling
emerald leaves
A soft dusky sheer curtain adds a glow to the sparkling after-rain sheen
Parking the car beneath a branching proud oak
Then walking down the dry cement walk beneath shady wide maples
Entering the school which never looked so mystic before
The yellow brick surrounded by new dark velvety grass and tall swaying
trees
Down the hall you walk, enchanted as you breathe the air of corsages
of roses, orchids, or what-have-you
Depositing your coat and admiring your own sky-blue billowy gown
decorated with tiny pink flowers and your very own first corsage
Glancing proudly at your escort, so tall and handsome in his dark blue
suit and white carnation
Couples pass by you, all smiling and enchanted, all happy in their
youthful exuberance

Page two (The Prom)

Then down the stairs, as the walls echo, "Lucky you. I'm lucky, too.
Wonder what the evening holds for you?"
At last you breathe a sigh as your eyes fall on the beautifully decorated
ballroom
Once the gymnasium but not now. You're in a nightclub, and there's
the orchestra. Everything looks as you had dreamed and hoped for.
Still breathless you glide out to the crowded dance floor, your new white
shoes aching to keep time with the soft slow music
In the arms of your escort, you float on a cloud, in a dream filled with
soft lights, a crepe paper ceiling, the skylights of New York, the
audience of couples, stag lines, and wallflowers watching wistfully
Gowns of silk, organdy, satin and rayon
Colors of mint, apple blossom pink, soft yellow, crystal white, deep
green and powder blue
Billowing, rustling, flowing (but you like yours the best!)
All too soon the time passes
After refreshments of pretzels, cokes, cookies, and mints, the crowd
thins out
It's getting late. Time to leave
You watch sadly as the evening draws to a close. The last dance, the
falling crepe paper, the clinging dancers, the low lights
Gentle hands place your wrap around your shoulders
Repeating goodbyes, then walking slowly down the steps, down the
walk, beneath the mystic dark trees, into the car
The evening closes, altogether with darkness.

Later, as you sink wearily beneath the soft blankets, you dream.
The night is over. All you have are memories, memories,
a wilted corsage, a tiny bit of crepe paper, your ticket,
and memories, memories, which you will treasure forever.

Spring

The world is a bubble of sunshine and light
When it's spring.
The world is blossomed in pink and in white
When it's spring
The world is an orchestra sending its tune
When it's spring
The world is a happy place, then all too soon,
Spring leaves.

Weather

Weather, why are you so cruel and changeable?
You let the grass begin to sprout
Then you let their roots freeze out
You let the birds come early hither
Then you keep them in a dither
As you change from hot to cold
Your mischievousness won't go untold!

The Tortoise and the Hare

It seems to me that race between
the tortoise and the hare
has yet not found a finish line
to end. For, if I dare,
I notice that the hare has sent
his son to follow through
in hopes that he won't tend to lag
like he, himself, did do!

Who Knows?

What holds the hushed new morning
what holds the darkened night
what holds the earth spellbound
as travels a bird in flight?
What holds the sun so breathless
what holds the vast blue sky
what holds the clouds of fury
so very high yet nigh?
Who knows when the moment is here
who knows of the time gone by
who knows of the future before us
how we're here and why?
Mysteries bury the doorstep
blanket our mind with snow
for who, my good man, should answer
that only our Great Father knows.

≫⊚ ⊚≪
Chapter 26
≫⊚ ⊚≪

Songs

Although Brigitta and Mary grew up appreciating their German heritage, they regretted the inability to bond with grandparents in Germany who they never got to meet due to World War II separating the continents. Also, there were aunts, uncles and cousins whom they never got to meet, as well. A few aunts did correspond regularly, but for the most part, there was a silence due to the War.

Letters that were allowed to arrive from Germany were mostly always read and censored before they reached the United States.

Both girls treasured the birthday cards that they did receive, even though, in some cases, they were unable to decipher the German script. Their parents tried to help them as much as they could by translating things for them.

Sometimes the packages that Brigitta's mother sent to family in Germany never arrived or if they did, some of the items were removed before they received them. Life was very hard for their relatives in Germany during and after the War; therefore they much appreciated whatever food or clothing that was sent.

Brigitta's parents tried hard to preserve as much of their heritage as they could. Brigitta remembers a German folksong that her parents had taught her when she was little. She never forgot it. The title was "Hanschen klein."

Hanschen klein

Hanschen klein ging allein	Little Hans went alone
in die weite Welt hinein.	Out into the wide world.
Aber Mutter weinet sehr	but mother cries a lot
hat ja nun kein Hanschen mehr	Hasn't got a little boy anymore!
Da besinnit sich das Kind	Look! The child changes his mind
lauft nach haus geschwind.	And returns home quickly.

The words to the song differ depending upon who is doing the translating. Also, there are more verses and even more lines in some of them. But Brigitta and Mary only memorized the first verse as written above. For many years Brigitta thought the last line meant that the little boy never returned home again, and that made her sad.

At Christmastime both of her parents sang *Silent Night* together in German. Also, *O Tannenbaum* which means O Christmas tree.

Stille Nacht	Silent Night
Stille Nacht, heilige Nacht!	Silent Night, holy night.
Alles schlaft, einsam wacht	All is calm. All is bright.
nur das traute hoch-heilige Paar.	Round yon Virgin Mother and Child
Holder Knabeim lokkigen Haar	Holy infant so tender and mild
schlaf in himmlischer Ruh	Sleep in heavenly peace
schlaf in himmlischer Ruh.	Sleep in heavenly peace.

Inge Logenburg Kyler

O Tannenbaum	O Christmas Tree
O Tannenbaum, O Tannenbaum	O Christmas Tree, O Christmas Tree,
wie treu sind deine Blatter!	Thy leaves are so unchanging
O Tannenbaum, O Tannenbaum	O Christmas Tree, O Christmas Tree,
wie treu sind deine Blatter!	Thy leaves are so unchanging.
Du grunst nicht nur zur Sommerzeit	Not only green when summer's here
nein, auch im Winter wenn es schneit	but also when 'tis cold and drear.
O Tannenbaum, O Tannenbaum,	O Christmas tree, O Christmas tree
wie treu sind deine Blatter!	Thy leaves are so unchanging.

Chapter 27

An Allegheny Mountain
Boy Grows Up

Memories from Brigitta's Boyfriend, Arthur J. Kyler
The following stories are exactly as written by Arthur:

Part I

As a young lad, I always respected and looked up to my Granddad Emil
and Grandma Josephine. Emil and Josephine were my mother's parents.
I was always closer to my mother's side of the family, not that I didn't
respect my dad's family, but that is another story for another day.

I always remember Granddad as a very religious man (Christian
Missionary Alliance), a small church on Merrill Street in Clearfield, Pa.
Granddad always sat in the front row in church and when the pastor
said something that inspired him, he would speak right out, saying
"Praise the Lord, Amen."

Granddad would go to the Clearfield jail house and talk to the
prisoners and pray for the prisoners to try and change their way of
life. I remember when some people would come out to the farm when
Granddad would be working in the fields. He would stop working and
sit down, talk and pray with them.

Granddad told me a few stories of his younger days, as he would

77

say "Before I met the Lord and got saved." When he was in his early twenties, he decided to get rich and go for the gold in Alaska. He teamed up with an Old Man, I do not know his name, in the late 1800's, going by train heading north to Nome, Alaska.

Along the way there was all kinds of material that people had discarded so they could continue on. How he finally got there, I do not know. He said they camped along "water's edge in tents" and paned for gold in the cold weather. But he never got rich! On the way back home, at one time, they had to travel across a large bay in a real bad storm in Alaska. Hour by hour they rowed in fear of the boat capsizing. His hands got sore and raw from the strain of paddling. I assume they traveled back home by train once they got back to land.

Granddad lived through the Prohibition time. He drove brewery wagons, delivering beer, whiskey and such. He showed me cock rooster spurs they used for rooster fights. People would bet on whose rooster would win.

I'm not sure when my Godin Grandparents got married. They lived on a small farm in a town called Madera, near Houtzdale, PA. One day lightning struck the barn and burned it down. Granddad then bought an approximately two-hundred-acre farm in Mt. Joy, PA. The address: was Emil Godin, Mt. Joy Rd#4, Clearfield, Pennsylvania.

This farm is where I recall some of my childhood days growing up. There were nine siblings in the Godin family: Uncle Lewis, Uncle Amos, Uncle Paul, Aunt Fannie, Aunt Divine, Aunt Rachael, Aunt Daisy, and, of course, my mother Josephine. Josephine married my father, Emerson Kyler. They are all now deceased. One sibling, Aunt Mary, died in infancy.

The first house I remember we lived in the Allegheny Mountains of Pennsylvania was on the corner of Mt. Joy and Goshen Road. Granddad

Godin helped my dad build the house. It had a large kitchen with a big cooking stove that we burned coal in for heat and cooking.

There was a smaller living room with a heating stove in it. There were two bedrooms upstairs, one for Mom and Dad, and one for us kids.

We did not have indoor plumbing, but used an outhouse out back. We had a well outside with a winch rope on it. You hooked a bucket on the winch rope and dropped it into the well to get water.

When we lived there, I remember my mom loved to go on picnics. So she would pack a picnic lunch and we would walk down the green field over the hill to a nice little creek that ran down through the valley. The birds would be singing, and mom would lay out a blanket and we would spend the afternoon there. At that time there were just three of us: Marjorie, Dallis and me. I don't think Violet was born yet, but she might have been. That was so much fun for me.

This is where we lived when I started to go to school in the first grade. This was during the Depression Years. My dad worked for the WPA (Works Progress Administration, part of the New Deal formed in 1935 and dissolved in 1943) busting up rocks to build roads nearby for a minimum wage of $2.00 a day.

I went to a one-room school, 6 grades; grade 1 though 6th. This was in the Mt. Joy Schoolhouse. I still remember my first day of school in the first grade. Our teacher's name was Mrs. Schaffer. When I walked in the school, the teacher said, "find your desk with your name across the top." This was a challenge since we really didn't know how to read or write yet.

But it didn't take long till we were reading the First Grade Primer and starting to write cursive. Nobody talked during school classes. We had two recesses; one in the morning and one in the afternoon when you bundled up and went outside to play for fifteen minutes, plus a lunch hour. We played different games at lunch hour and recess. (Red Rover to Balls Coming Over), and, of course, we boys always played Cowboys with our toy pistols strapped to our sides (Roy Rogers, Gene Autry, etc.)

I went to school lst and 2nd grade in the Mt. Joy School about ten miles from Clearfield, PA in the middle of farming country. There were about six small two-hundred-acre dairy farms in this area, including granddad's farm. They all had about ten to twelve dairy cows each. I remember going to the barn early in the morning (before school) with kerosene lanterns, usually three lanterns, and hanging them up behind the twelve cows that were in stanchion.

It was always warm in the barn because the cows gave off a lot of heat. I remember my dad and granddad sitting on the three-legged milking stool and filling the milk bucket full of milk, milking by hand. When the milk bucket got full, they walked to the milk-house and put the milk through a strainer into five-gallon milk cans. We would get three to four cans of milk in the evenings and three to four cans in the mornings, always milking twice a day, early in the morning and about 4 o'clock in the evening. In the morning the full milk cans were taken to the Dairy in Clearfield.

After all twelve cows were milked, we would unhook the stanchion around their necks and let them out to pasture in the summer in a field that was too steep to farm. In the wintertime they were released into a big shed and fenced-in-yard.

We had a dog named Trixie. Around 4 o'clock, we would say, "Trixie, bring in the cows!" She would go to the pasture field and slowly herd all the cows back to the barn. Every cow had its own stanchion, and they knew which one was theirs. If a new cow went into the wrong stanchion, the resident cow of that stanchion would shove that cow out and it had to find its own stanchion.

We had a large silo that was filled full of silage (which was chopped up corn that kind of fermented in the silo, stalks and all while it was green). Each cow would get a basket full of the silage (silage or ensilage, we called it), and a cup full of chop (ground up corn and commercial chop), some chopped up beets (that was in a big bin in front of the cows), then a cup of molasses syrup on top of that! They loved that meal!

Then later, after milking, we would fork in hay to the trough in front of them for the evening. Each cow had a gravity water bowl by each side so they would put their noses in and push down, and water would run in for them to drink. This water came from a large cistern (like a well) on top of the hill that the windmill pumped to it.

The cows always had fresh straw in the stanchion area for bedding. There was a long trough that ran behind all the cows that was about two feet wide and about ten inches deep that the cows would poop and pee in during the night. After the cows were left out in the morning the trough had to be cleaned out and new bedding put down for the evening. There was a large manure carrier that ran on a rail from the ceiling that we pushed along and shoveled the manure into it, then shoved it out the side door into the big manure pit in the wintertime or dump it into the manure spread that was outside the door.

The manure carrier had a handle on it that we would pull when we got it to where we wanted it to be dumped. It would turn upside down and dump everything out. I was always fascinated by the way it worked.

In the fall when the corn was still green on the stalk (corn stalks and all), the local farmers would all get together and go from one farm to another and fill all the silos. They all had a team of horses pulling a flat wagon. The corn would be cut by hand with small hand scythes and laid flat across the wagon beds.

When the wagon was full, they pulled it to the silo where there was a big silo filler. The silo filler was run by a tractor that had a big pulley on the side of it. A large belt went from the tractor to the pulley on the silo filler. The silo filler had a conveyor belt that was about 15 or 20 ft. long and a large cutting wheel that chopped up the corn and blew it up a long set of pipes to the top of the silo. This process would continue until the silo was full.

Meanwhile, the women would be in grandma's summer kitchen preparing a large meal for all the workers. In the summertime after the corn was planted and it was starting to grow, grandpa Emil Godin would cultivate the corn to keep the weeds down. The cultivator would be hooked behind our big white horse called Jim. (Grandpa had a team of white horses). Grandpa would walk behind, holding the handles on the cultivator between the rows. I had to ride on the horse and steer it so it would not step on any of the rows of corn. My butt would get to hurting sometimes from bumping up and down! But it worked okay!

We also grew a large field of beets and turnips for the cows, and a big field of potatoes for winter. I had to walk the rows when the potatoes got big and pick off the potato bugs and throw them into a can I carried with me that had some fuel oil in it to kill the bugs. I never liked this job, but I did it anyway!

We had a large chicken coop with lots of chickens so we had plenty of eggs. When the chickens quit laying, usually it was in the winter time, we would butcher some. It was my job to lay them on a chopping block and cut off their heads, always making sure the first wack was a clear cut. I remember my mom and grandmother pulling the feathers and cleaning the chickens, then cutting them up into pieces and cooking them, then putting them up into canning jars for eating later.

In the spring time the mailman delivered baby chicks (called peeps) in big boxes. We had a small brooder house that the chicks were raised in until they got big enough to be put into the big chicken house. The chicken house was in one side of a big shed. Grandpa had a big forge in the other side of the shed where he would get a fire going to repair tools in the winter time.

We also raised wheat or oats to feed the animals in the winter. (cows, horses, chickens.) We never raised hogs (pigs) on the Godin farm, but they did on the Kyler farm, which I will discuss later when I get into memories from the Kyler farm in Shawville, Pa.

I lived on the Godin farm in different ages of my childhood. After my Grandma Godin died (I was about five years old), my aunts and uncles would take turns living on the farm to help Grandpa Godin with the farming chores (milking cows, harvesting crops, etc.).

One of the earliest memories of living on the farms, I was very young and my Uncle Paul and Aunt Julia were on the farm, I slept in a little room upstairs and sometimes would get scared...and Aunt Julia would let me sleep with her until I calmed down. (I was around 3 or 4 years old).

Those were during the Depression Years. My dad worked for the W.P.A. (Works Project Administration), making a minimum of about $2.00 a day. So my four sisters and I would stay with some of our aunts and uncles for a short spell, or at least until school started again.

I had one uncle (Uncle Amos) that I clearly remember when I was only five years old. He drove a big coal truck that he delivered coal from the coal mines to the coal tipples where it was dumped in a big coal shoot that went into the big train cars at the mine. I rode with him, one day, and it was very exciting!

We stopped in the town of Curwensville for lunch (where he lived at that time) and Aunt Ruth (his wife) had a lunch ready for us.

Uncle Amos went away to a big city to work for a while. I think it was Cleveland, Ohio. He got mixed up with some bad company as far as I can figure out and ended up with some kind of disease. The doctor scared him into believing he could not get cured (I was about five years old). He took a gun and killed himself in the old corn crib on the farm.

I remember his funeral in grandma's house. Her house had a large kitchen and living room downstairs with four bedrooms upstairs. There was a room off the living room called the parlor. Grandpa called it the "Prayer Room."

I remember there was a big old pump organ in the room. Anyway, when someone passed away, the casket was put in this room for the funeral service. I remember going into the parlor where the casket was and putting my hands on the edge of it, and looked up at Uncle Amos's eyes, and a tear flowed down from the corner of his eye, telling me how sorry he was. It's too bad that people revert to this tragic thing to do. If they only realized how devastated it is to the rest of the family, but this is closure for this to me for now.

I have lot of memories of life on the Godin farm—that I'll get back to later. When I was in third or fourth grade, we moved to a little town called LaJose, PA, where my dad (Emerson Kyler) took a job working for my Uncle Lewis Godin who had a coal stripping business. My dad was in charge of the coal tipple where the coal trucks would bring the coal to dump into the big coal tipple that filled the train coal cars (as mentioned earlier). I was about eight years old. I had four sisters: Marjorie (ten); Dallis (six); Violet (four), and Shirley (one).

I remember one day when we lived in LaJose, just before Christmas time, I walked into the livingroom and my mom was sitting on the couch, crying. I said, "Mom, what is the matter?" She looked at me with tearful eyes and said, "Oh Art, it is Christmas time and there isn't enough money to buy presents for everyone, and I wanted to buy dollies for the girls." I said, "Mom, don't worry about me!"

Mom bought me a little Boy Scout kind of a knife that I really cherished! That was the nicest Christmas that I can remember!

I went to a small country school in LaJose for the 3rd and 4th grade. Me and a group of boys at lunch time ran down to our favorite swimming hole. The school bell always rang twice at noon. The first ring meant you had 15 minutes to get back to school before the 2nd bell would ring. On this day, we didn't hear the first, bell, so when the 2ndbell rang, we thought it was the 1st bell. When we ran back to school, we were late, of course, and the teacher was very upset, so we couldn't go swimming at noon anymore!

After two years, my Uncle Lewis Godin's coal business had financial problems, so we had to move back to the Clearfield, PA, area again, to a house on the corner of Mt. Joy Road and Goshen Road. The address was Mt. Joy R.D.#1, Clearfield, PA. When we had moved to LaJose, dad sold this house to Aunt Alva, who was Uncle Lewis's wife. They had two children, Eddie and Mona Godin, who were my cousins. Alva turned the lower walkout basement into a neat little store that she kept up for a few years.

So we moved back onto Grandpa Godin's farm for a few years and I went back to the Mt. Joy one room school for 5th and 6th grades. My sister Marjorie and Dallis were at the school, also. We always walked to school. I remember one winter day when we were walking home to the farm and it began to snow hard. I took a shortcut through the fields to get home quicker with my younger sister Dallis. She had a hard time walking, so I put her on my back. She was crying. I said, "don't worry! We'll get home okay, and did, of course.

The old schoolhouse is still there today and is being used for a community building. There is a Methodist Church next to it that is still active today.

Dad worked the farm with Grandpa Godin. There wasn't much money but it got food on the table. When I was in 6th grade they decided to move the 6th graders into a bigger school (Plymptonville Elementary). I think there were six of us. We kind of stayed to ourselves at recess and lunchtime, and didn't seem to fit in with the other students. So after about two weeks of this, they moved us back to the Mt. Joy country school. We were happy, but the teacher was little bit upset, but it worked out okay.

When we went to 7th grade, then we had to go to the big junior high school in Clearfield, but we were ready for it by that time. 7Th, 8th and 9th grades were in the junior high school. 10Th, 11th and 12th grades were in the big high school across the street from the junior high school.

Once I got into the 10th grade I chose the Carpentry and Cabinet Making Shop. We would spend one week in the shop class in the tech school and one week in the big high school for social studies, math, English and history, switching back and forth. We had drafting classes in the shop class, studying and drafting blueprints for house construction.

Around this time, about 1951, my mother had a Surprise! She was 40 years old, and with child. That is when my brother, Daniel E. Kyler, was born.

(When Inge and I were married in 1954, Danny was about 4 years old.)

For my senior year I built a full-size desk for my Senior Project, which turned out nice. When I moved to Michigan, my sister Dallis kept the desk for a good many years.

Now, back to the memories of my Grandpa Godin's farm in Mt. Joy, countryside, Clearfield, PA. One day we had a big wind storm. This was when we were living at what is called the cross roads of Mt. Joy and Goshen Roads, and Aunt Julia lived next door. She ran into our house, and said "Pap (Grandpa Godin) has been hurt." He tried to close the big barn door when the wind was blowing real hard and it came off of the hinges and fell on him, breaking his leg. An ambulance took him to the hospital to repair his leg. He always limped after that but recovered okay. This all happened before we moved to LaJose when my dad worked for Uncle Lou Godin as a coal tipple operator.

Before then, my dad (Emerson Kyler) was working in the Clearfield brickyards making thousands of bricks for building houses, etc. He said he was sorry he left that job to go into the coal mining business, but after a while, the brickyard closed down anyway.

When I was in high school, 11th and 12th grades, I met my high school sweetheart, Inge Logenburg. She would walk down the street (the high school and junior high school were both in downtown Clearfield) to Woodies Gas Station after school (where I worked) to meet me. The man who owned the gas station was called Woodie. He owned an old green Plymouth pickup. I'd say to Woodie "can I take my girlfriend home in the pickup," and he said, "Yeah, I guess so," so I'd put in 25cents worth of gas. It was an old truck (gas was 25cents a gallon then) and take my girlfriend home. Inge had a girlfriend, Ellen Carns, and I had a school friend named John Kolbe, so the four of us would go out together sometimes. We had lots of fun together. This was the time when my Aunt Daisy and Uncle Vic Chnupa were living on Grandpa Godin's farm. Inge and I would drive out to visit them in the big old farmhouse.

One evening after we visited them, it was late, so I thought I better be getting Inge home. She lived with her parents in what was called Wolf Run, Clearfield, Pa. I decided to take a shortcut to Wolf Run. It was springtime, and the shortcut road was a muddy dirt road! When we were going down the hill, my wheels got into a rut that took us off the road and almost over the hill (and into a creek!) I had my dad's car, a 1948 blue Kaiser, a nice car. So we got out of the car and walked down the road and walked (in the mud) to the nearest house. Inge had nice clothes on and we got kind of muddy.

When we got to the first house we came to, I knocked on the door and a man came and I told him how I was stuck. He said "no problem! I'll get you out." He had an old Model A Ford, I think it was. He took us back to the stuck car and hooked a chain on the bumpers and pulled us out. The mud was flying all over us and the car but I finally got my girlfriend back home. She probably got heck for getting home late!

When I worked at Woodie's Gas Station on 3rd street in Clearfield, my dad worked part-time at a Bar (St. Charles Cafe) across the street, owned by Dan Spingola. Dad tended the bar and cooked small orders, mostly hamburgers and such. I would go across the street and dad would cook me up a delicious hamburger! I pumped gas, greased and washed cars. We repaired big truck tires that got flat. They were huge tires! I don't know how I handled them, but I did.

Another friend of mine, George Collar, also worked at Woodie's. We decided to go West to maybe Oregon to look for a job. Meanwhile, my girlfriend's dad, Bill Logenburg, went to Lansing, Michigan and got a good job at the Oldsmobile Plant, and told us (George and I) that there was a lot of work in Lansing. So we quit Woodie's and headed West, and stopped in Lansing..and that is as far West as we got!

We got a construction job. My girlfriend (Inge Logenburg) and I got married October 30, 1954. We had three lovely children: Heidi, Steven, and Glenn.

Part II – **Kyler Homestead:** Memories (as remembered and written by Arthur J. Kyler)

I am now going to recall some memories of the Kyler Homestead in Shawville, PA. The Kyler family that lived on the farm in Shawville, about twenty miles from Clearfield, PA, had eight siblings as follows:

Emerson Kyler (Josephine) My parents
Uncle Walter Kyler (Aunt Francine)
Uncle Millard Kyler (Aunt Hope)
Uncle Austle Kyler (Aunt Mable)
Uncle Lewis Kyler (Aunt Cora)
Aunt Margaret Kyler McCracken (Uncle Ward)
Aunt Bertha (Kyler) Graham (Uncle Don)
Aunt Esther (Kyler) Kephart (Uncle Boyd

My Grandpa Henry Kyler died when I was quite young. I remember going to the Kyler farm to visit once (when I was quite young), and he was sick in bed and died shortly after that. My Grandma Kyler died when my dad (Emerson) was about 8 years old, so my dad (Emerson) only went to the third grade in school as he had to stay home to help with household chores.

When my dad and mother first married, from what I recall, they lived at the Kyler homestead for a short time. One day when my dad (Emerson) went hunting on the steep side of the mountain by the farm, his shotgun started to slip down the hill. When he reached out to grab it, the gun hit a rock and caused it to discharge. Dad was reaching out with his right arm, and the discharge hit part of the inside of his arm. Fortunately, his arm healed up okay, but there was always a couple of shot pellet under the skin of his arm.

Around this time, my parents moved to a little town in Stockton, New York, and dad worked on a farm there and that is where I was born March 3, 1934. Then we moved back to Clearfield soon after that.

The road that went from Clearfield to Shawville was called Shawville Road. (Shawville was a small rural community). The road wound around and up and down the mountain side as it went up one side of the mountain to the top where my Aunt Margaret McCracken and Uncle Walter lived. You could look way down the side of the mountain to the bottom where the Wet Branch of the Susquehanna River ran right past the Kyler Homestead of about two hundred acres, and you could see the whole farm, the big white farmhouse, big barn and several sheds and outbuildings.

All the siblings eventually married off and moved off of the farm except my Uncle Millard and Aunt Hope. They raised a couple of milk cows and several pigs (hogs) for butchering in the fall. Uncle Millard had a good-sized smokehouse that they would smoke and cure the hog hams, bacon, etc. I always liked to smell the good smells coming out of the smokehouse.

Thanksgiving time was always time to butcher the hogs and prepare the meat for wintertime. I spent a couple summers at the Kyler homestead in Shawville with my cousin Homer Kyler. We did a lot of farm chores such as milking the cows, feeding the pigs, etc. Aunt Hope always made butter from the milk from the cows. The buttermilk, I thought, was very delicious, that Aunt Hope stored in the Spring House (a separate building for such). The extra buttermilk went to the pigs.

Uncle Millard Kyler also owned a coal business called Kyler Coal Company. It consisted of a couple of coal mines off the Shawville Road by the little Shawville community by Stone Creek (Stone Creek Road). My dad worked for my Uncle Millard's coal company for a few years. He was a Tipple Foreman and worked the tipple by himself. It was quite a sophisticated operation, I thought. The big coal trucks would back up a ramp and dump their load of coal in the big shoot at the top of the tipple. Dad worked below it by a large conveyor system. He would turn the upper conveyor belt on and the coal would come down the big coal shoot onto the conveyor belt and dad would pick out all the boney, they called it, (rocks and shale) and throw it out a discard shoot.

The coal then would go through a large crusher that crushed it into smaller pieces and continue on out on another conveyor that ran out to dump into the big railroad cars. When one part of the railroad car got full, dad would go down to move it. That was quite amazing to me, also, dad would crawl up a big ladder on the back of the railroad car and turn a big wheel at the top that unlocked the brake on the railroad car. He then crawled down the ladder and placed a big jack under the back wheel and pushed down on it until the coal car started to move. Then he would hurriedly climb back up the ladder and turn the big wheel to lock the brakes again. That was amazing that he had to do this all by himself! I was tired and all covered with coal dust when I went home that day.

My Aunt Esther Kephart owned a little grocery store in Shawville. It also was the local post office that she ran. I went to work a few times with my dad and he would drop me off at Aunt Esther's store, and I would spend the day there helping her in the store. I liked that. It was fun for me!

There was another coal company in Shawville called the Lingle Coal company that my dad worked for a few years. This coal company was a strip mining company. The owner's name was Ben Lingle. Dad drove fuel truck for him, going around to different strip mines to fuel up all the drag line machines, bull dozers, etc.

Ben Lingle owned lots of land around there. He had a big private hunting lodge where he would bring in clientele during hunting season to stay and hunt. My dad was a great cook and when Ben had all those people in, dad, alone, did all the cooking for them.

Conclusion of Childhood Memories of Art Kyler.

Dedicated to my Dear Loving Wife, Inge M. Kyler; daughter – Heidi Rose Paseka; son – Steven D. Kyler; son – Glenn A. Kyler.

Signed: *Arthur J. Kyler*

March 29, 2023

Post script: When Emerson Kyler (Art's dad) passed, February 12, 1971, Ben Lingle had his crew plow through the mountain's snowy roads with bulldozers all the way from Clearfield to the Eden Cemetery in Shawville so that the funeral procession could get through.

Books by the Author

Anteanus, Back to the Homeland, Brigitta -Little Girl in the Allegheny Mountains, Canus Lupus, Crickets are Chirping but No One Can Hear Them, Down in the Valley, Holt and Delhi Township (Images of America), Life with Nicholas, Make Me a Blessing, Man in Number Nine, Michigan Folktales and Ballads, Never Give Up, Passing Through America,

Nicholas and the Golf Course Cat, Observations (Snoi-tav-resbo), On to Cancun, Red Raspberries, Search for a House, Settling on this Old Farm, Song of the High Country, Sons and Daughters, Stories for Lilah, Tecumseh, The Stepping Stones, The Wind and the Wood, To Kancamugus and Back, To Neah Bay and Back, When Firewood Turns to Cotton.

Poems have been published in Golden Circle, Poetry Parade, Poets of Today, American Bard, Ithica – Michigan Newspaper, Poets of the Midwest, Flame Avalon Anthology, Woods Runner, Personal Broadcasts Stereo WEFG, Jean's Journal, Scimitar and Song, Poetry Unlimited, Orphic Lute, The Lyric, The Muse, Cyclotron, The Country Guide, Rhymes for the Very Young, Bardic Echoes, Spring Anthology of 1967, the Grit, POET, Hoosier Challenger, Creative Review, International Anthology of World Brotherhood and Peace, Cappers, Pennsylvania Prize Poems, Prize Poems of the Poetry Society of Michigan, Lansing Poetry Club History, Forty Salutes to Michigan Poets, D. H. Lawrence Anthology, Christmas with Kate, The Guild Anthology, Pennsylvania Poetry Society electronic newsletters—and numerous other collections and anthologies including Poetry Society Anthologies: Sing Then I

Must, Golden Song, Water Music, Michigan, Heart Songs, Anthology Nineteen-Ninety, I Hear the Song and It Wells in Me.

The author has received hundreds of citations and awards for poems, including the 2014 Ingham County Historical Commission Heritage Award; has edited various books; illustrated "Tell Me Mama"; has been writing a column for a local paper for over twenty-five years, and has authored a variety of articles for different publications.

Printed in the United States
by Baker & Taylor Publisher Services